vine and milk

Dom Fitzgerald

Over 100 Funny and Classical Vine Compilation

ISBN–10 : 1-948191-13-X

ISBN-13 : 978-1-948191-13-5

First Edition

Printed in the U.S.A

Dedicated to our fans and all vine lovers.

Table of Contents

hey, I'm Lesbian
i thought you were
american

miss Keisha

miss Keisha

miss Keisha

oh my fucking God

she fucking dead

next time you put your
fucking

hands on me imam fucking rip
off your

face

Bitch

what'd he do to you

cos he fuckin

Pushed me

hey Maria

want some

this bitch empty

Yeet

my name is Trey and

i have basketball tomorrow

i'm on point and I got two games

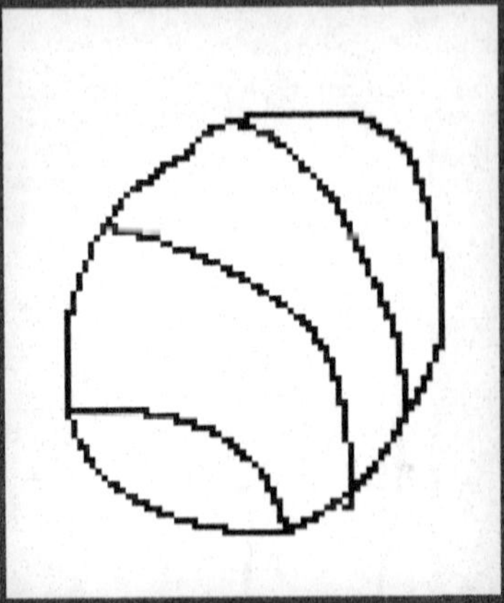

what the fuck is up Kyle
no what did you say
what the fuck dude
step the fuckup
kyle

you might not have been my
first love

but you were the love that
made all the other loves

irrelevant

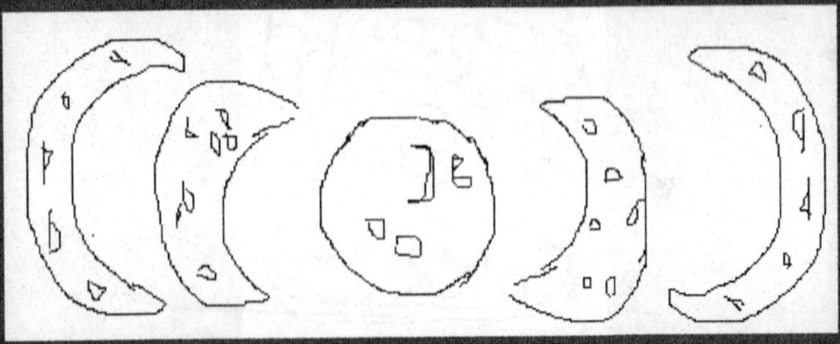

to make a long story

short

i shove a whole

bag of jellybeans

up my ass

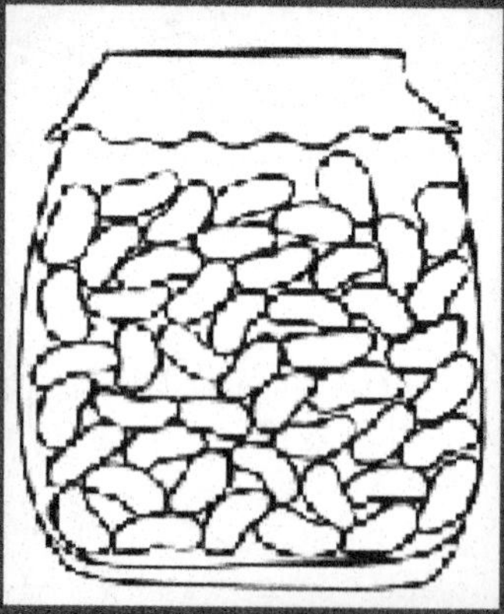

you were mine

and my life was full

you are no longer mine

and my life

is full

i'd be lying

if I said you make me

speechless

the truth is

you make my tongue so weak
it forgets what

language to speak in

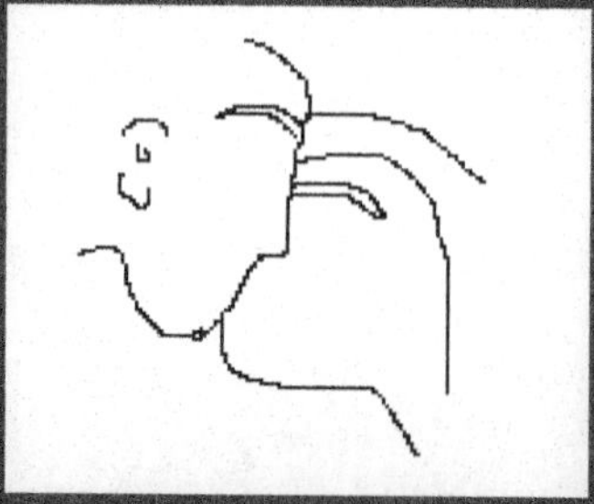

sometimes the apology
never comes

when it is wanted

and when it comes

it is neither wanted nor
needed

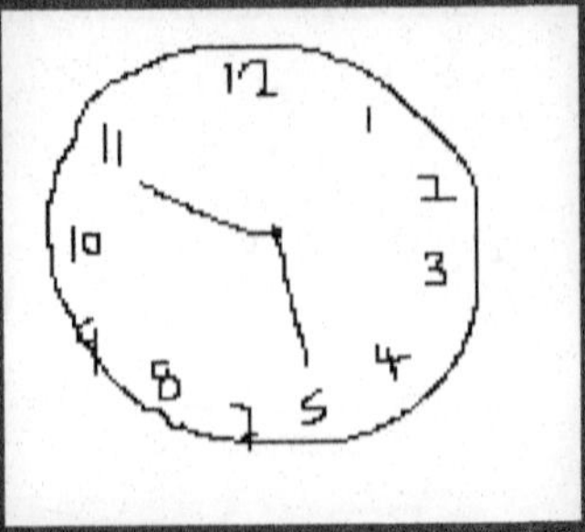

i don’t know what y’all

Ahh

you better stop

stop bitch

stop

Ahhh

dad why don't I have a car seat

because your hoe mother

fucked the pool boy jimmy

God

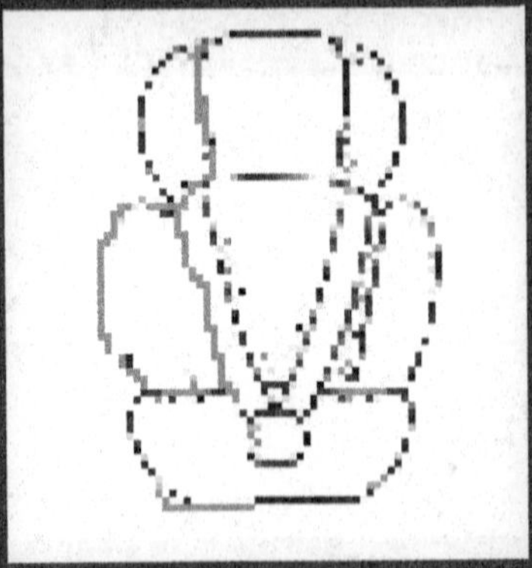

two bros chilling
in a hot tub
five feet apart
cause they aint gay

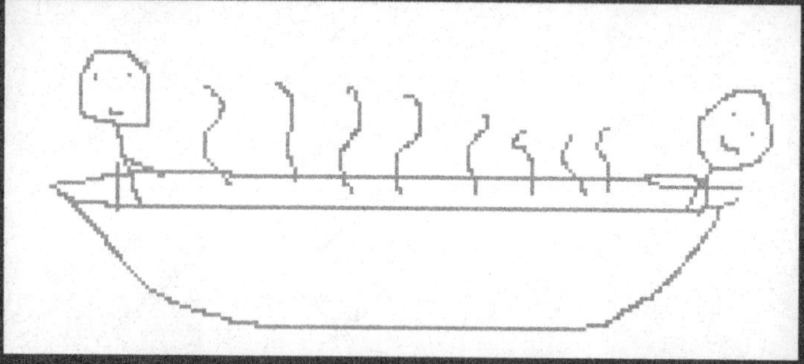

hi

welcome to chili's

has anyone ever told you

you look like beyonce

nah they usually tell me

i look like shalyssa

Who dafuq is shalyssa

Me

it's an avocado

thanks

have you ever had a dreams

that that you

Um

you had

you

you could

you do

you will

you wants

you

you do

so you

you do

you could

you

you want

you want tim

to do

you much you could do
anything

happy birthday bitch

so you gon bring me a
birthday gift

on my birthday

to my birthday party

with a birthday gift

i love you bitch

i ain't gonna stop loving you

B I T C H

whadup

I'm Jared

I'm 19 and

I never fuckin learned how to read

i do love working here

it's just

we all have a lot of laughs

Fuck off janet

I'm not going to your fucking

baby shower

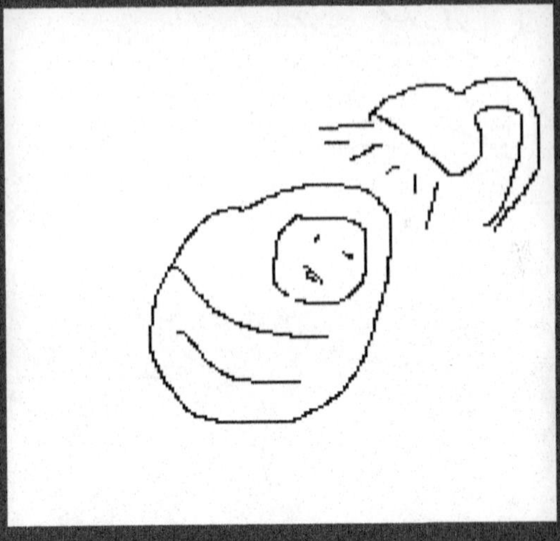

get to del taco

they got a new thing called

freesha-

freeshavacadoo

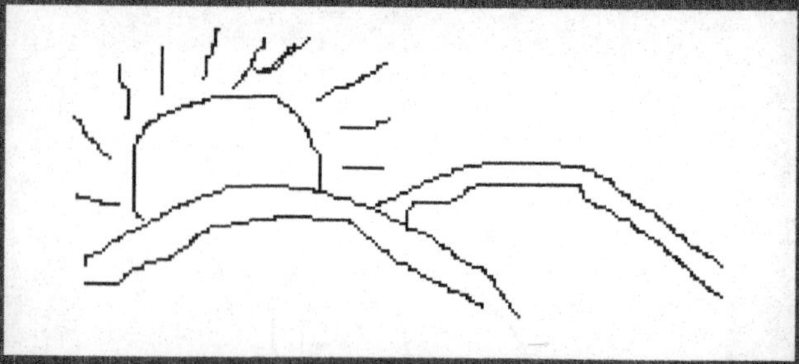

smile to the cam
bitch I hope the
fuck you do
you be a dead son of a bitch
i tell you that

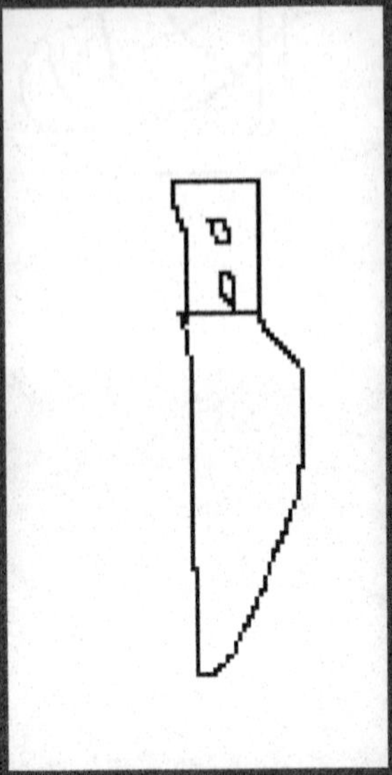

damn daniel

damn daniel

back at it again with the white vans

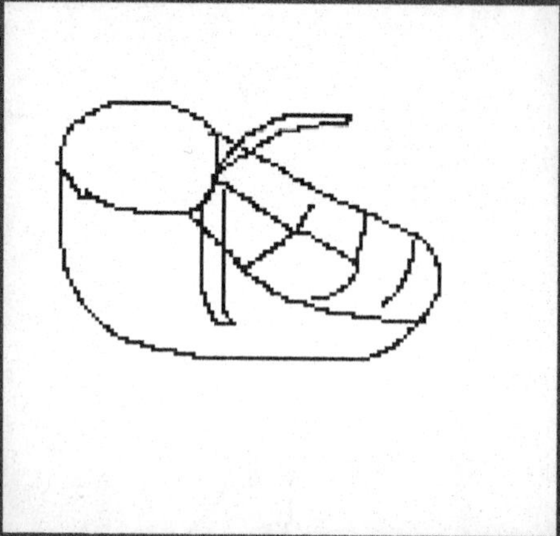

i wanna be a cowboy baby

you dance around

for fun

Laala

look at all those chickens

girl

you are thicker than

a bowl of oatmeal

that foo-foo lame shit

i aint wid it

i'll send some shots at your fitted

gra-ta-ta

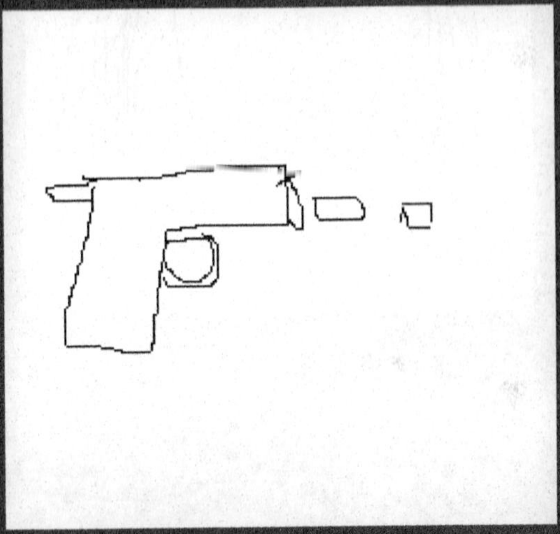

i'm not racists

or anything

but Asians

suuuuuuuucccccckkkkk

country boy

i love you

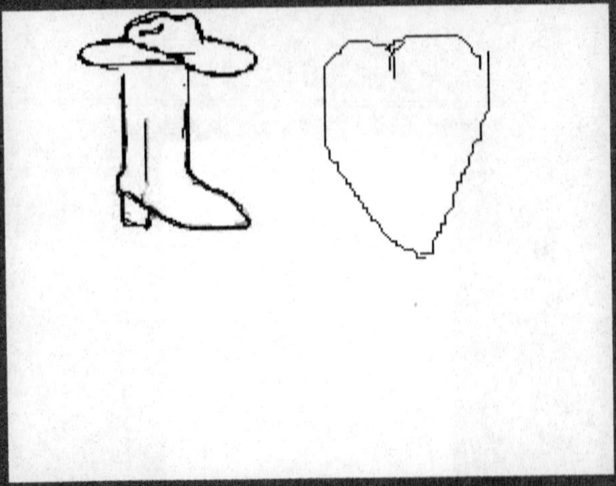

i spilled lipstick in your
valentino bag

you...whhhaa...lipstick in my
Valentino

shower time

glass of whiskey

and some denim jeans

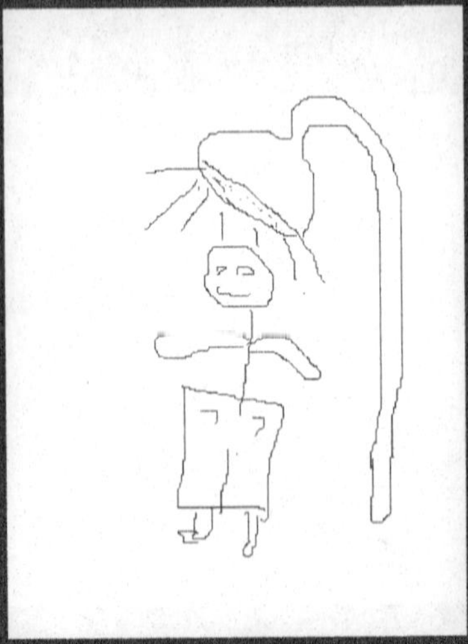

a potato flew

round my room

before you came

excuse the mess it made

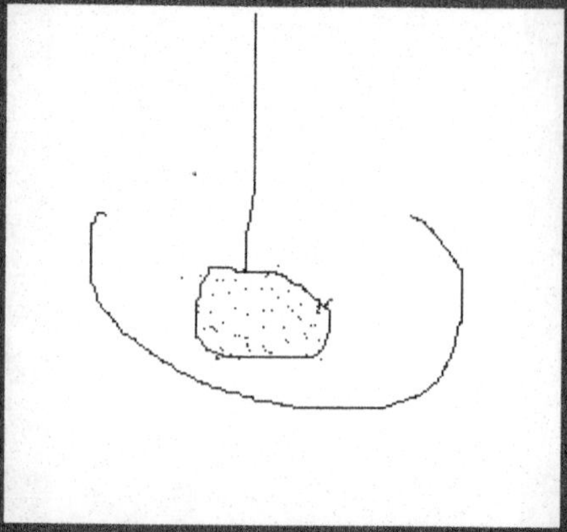

you freaking freaks
what would you want
what would you want
your actions have
consequences

my name is Jeff

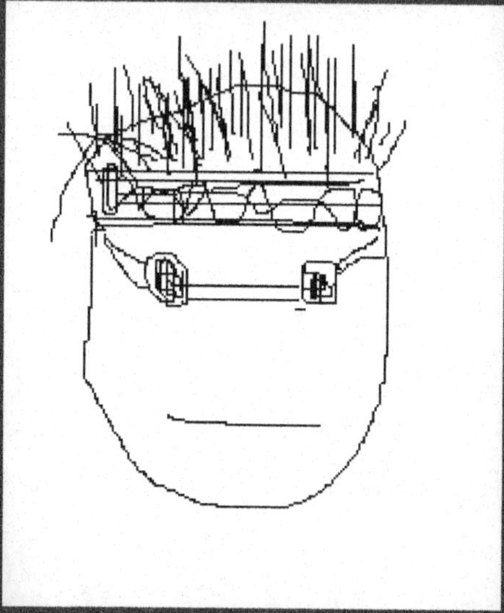

a lot of people are telling me

i'm like 2

nine years old

I'm eleven

so shut the fuck up

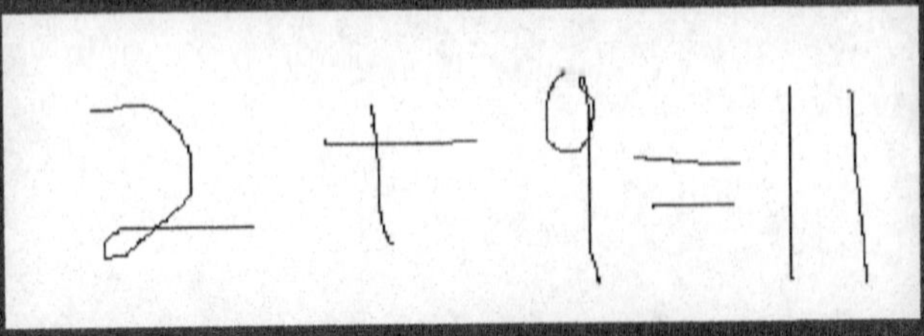

waddup people

i can shoot this

let's go

Arrrggghhhhhhh

daddy

do I look like your daddy?

i got a yes bitches
chuckle with a bit of swell
with a crunch please

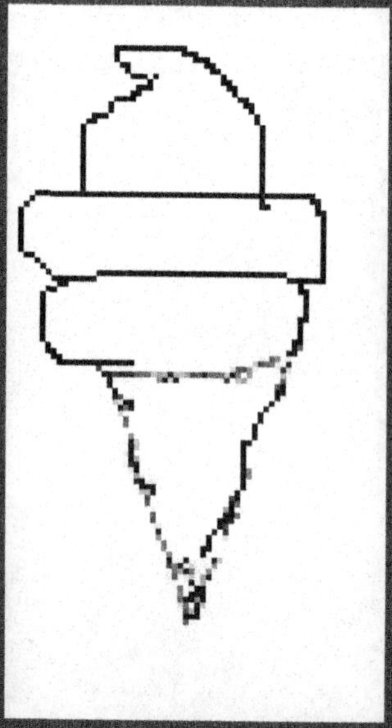

we are in this bitch

wanna get crunk

eye brows on Fleek

dafuq

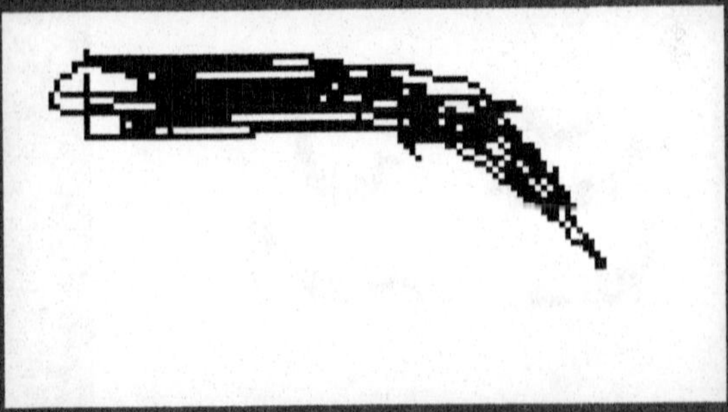

look at

look at

it's a freaking bat

i love Hogloween

excuse my party mouth

shut the fuck up

before a girl

gets her eye brows done

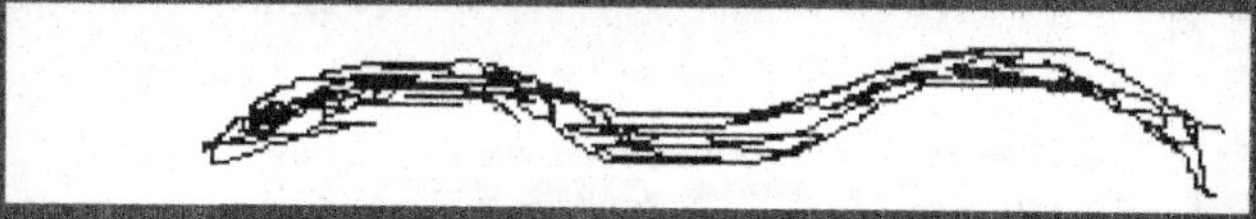

then after

"I'm a gross ass bitch"

happy new year

go to sleep

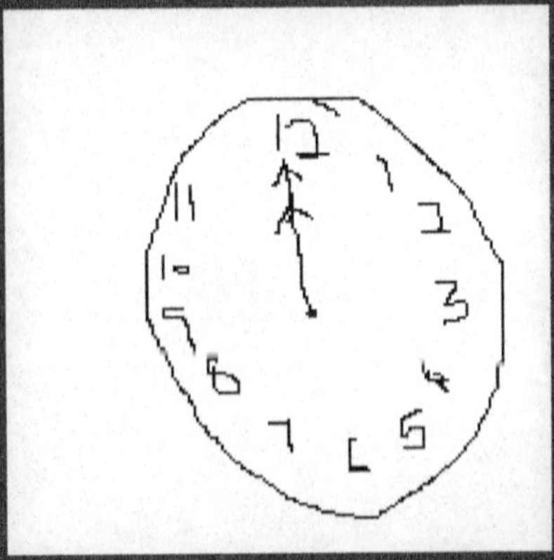

he cheated on me

let's go

i'm ready

whose driving

let me go get the cookie

fat ass

whatchu say

i said

dah ass

heyyy

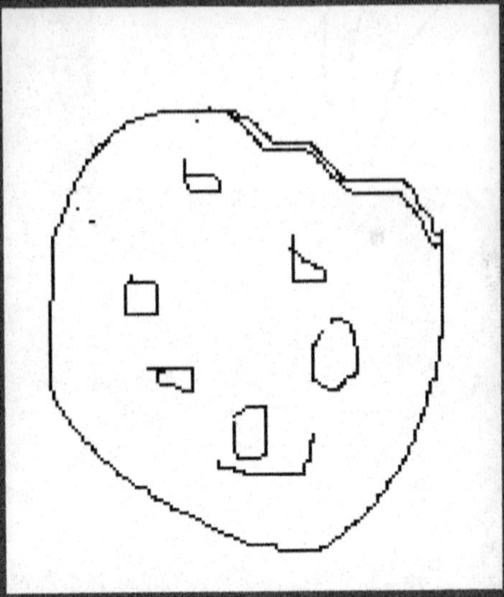

oh its your birthday

yeah

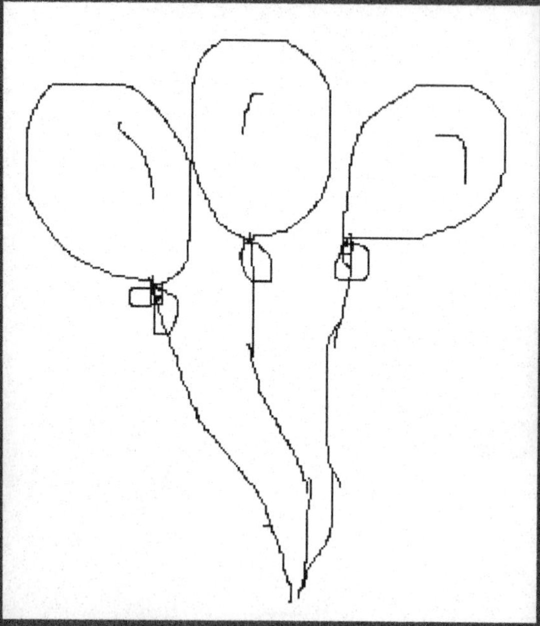

bitch get this off my face now

Oh

Oh

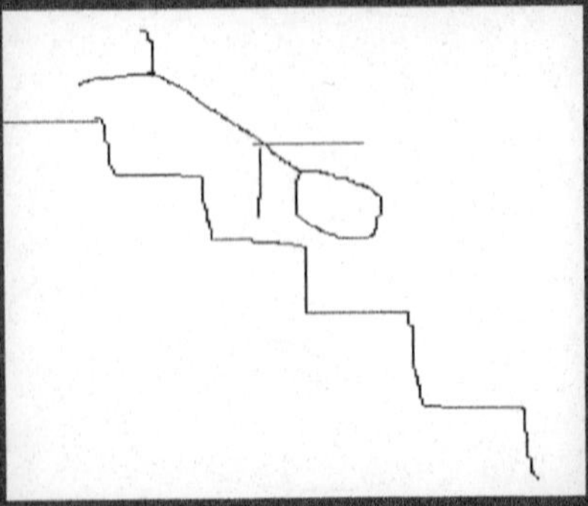

hahaha

babe why you like me

cos I just do

just a little bit more

you ready to go

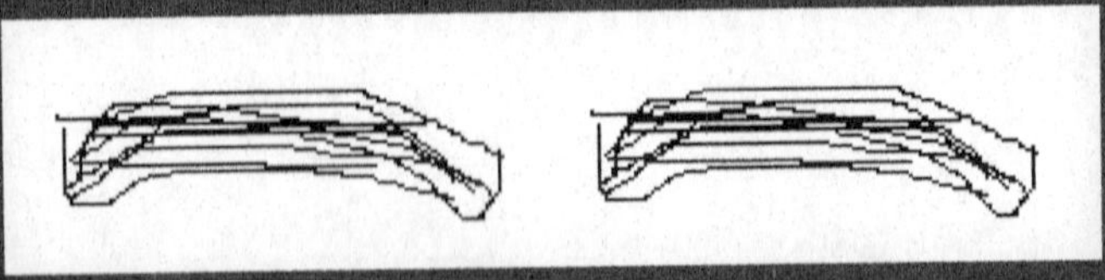

mum, I got to finish my eye
brows

happy valentine's day

oh white bear

i love it

happy valentine's day

Oh white girl

love it

i can't stop twerking

i can't stop twerking

i just can't

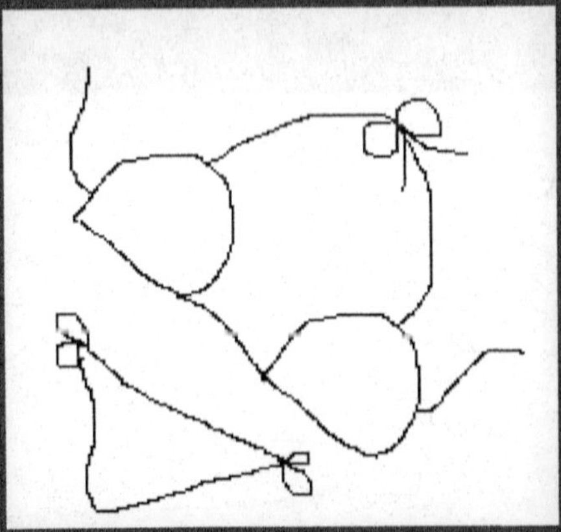

let's go to the mall

tomorrow

oh my gosh

hey baby

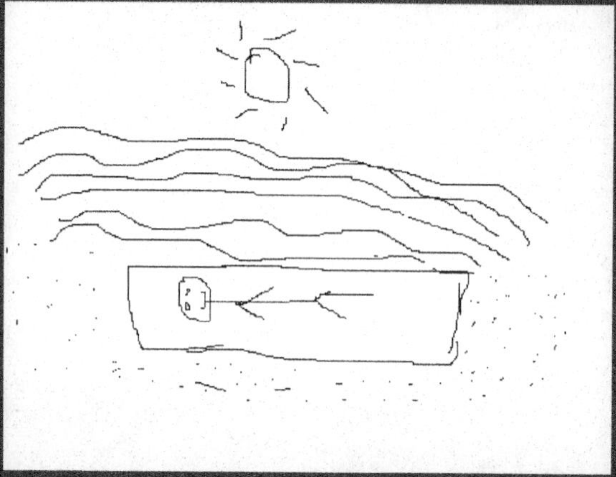

when he's mean to you

it means he likes you

i don't like you

i'm a dolphin

"ahck ahck ahck"

oh shit

i'm not good with girls

hi, wanna mate

i like your neck

you are so beautiful

fuck outta here

i brought this damn   thing for
you

that's sweet

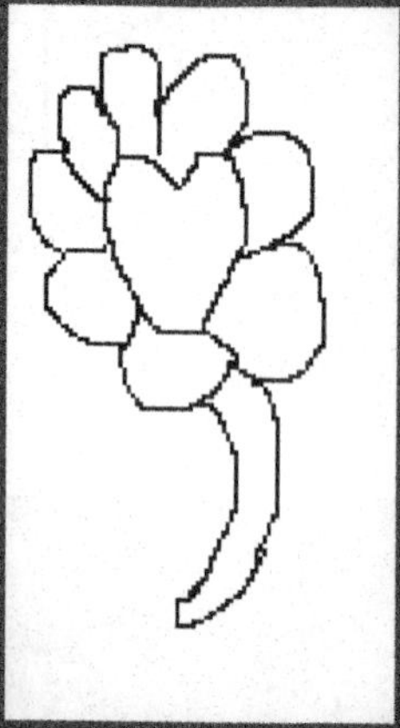

give me my hand back

c'mon

whaaat

selfiee

let me see

i don't like it

post it

delete the fucking picture

BECKY

so you going home

no

good night

you getting out bitch

c'mon bitch

i have no soul

i have none either

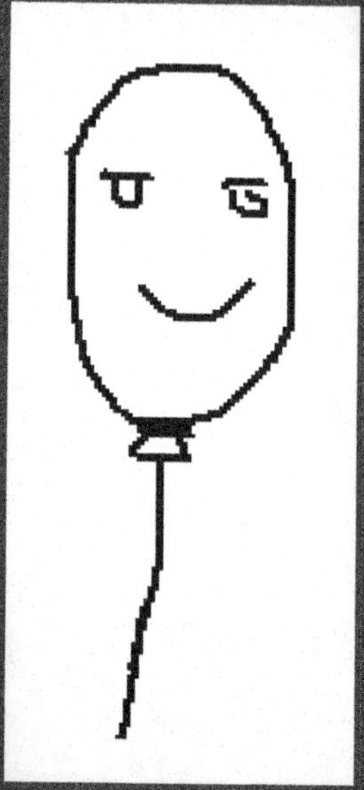

there's only one thing

worse than a rapist

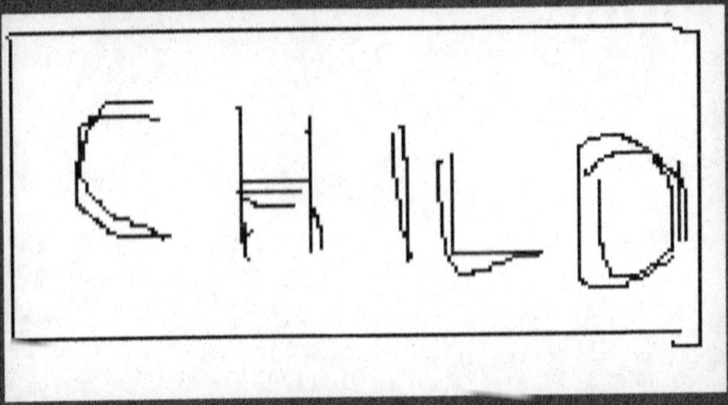

uh dude

ah suh dude

ahaha

aha suh dude

ahaha

Aarghhhh

yo stop

i could had dropped my croissant

i thought you were bae

turns out you just fam

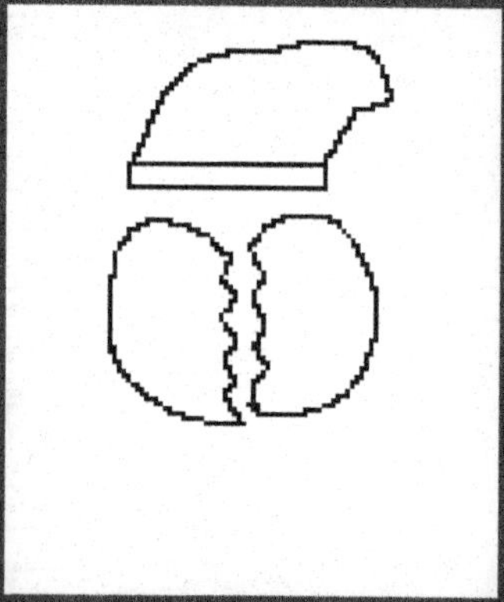

say cheese

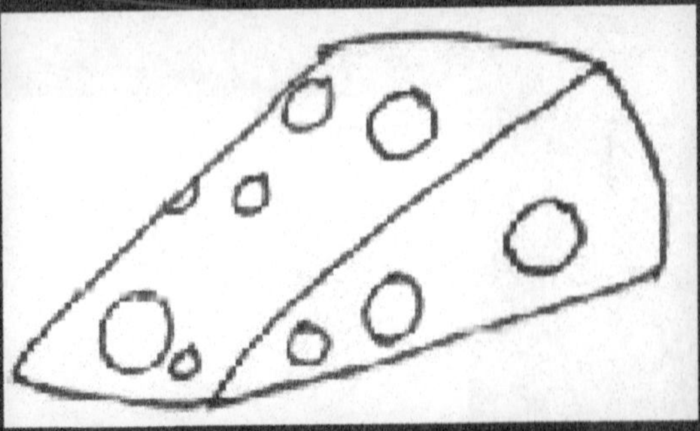

hungry nana

singing nana

squashed banana

whaat!

bang

this is why mum

doesn't freaking love you

its a fucking bear

arrgh

she's right there

i've heard that

this place is haunted

a 9-year old girl died here

"I'm eleven"

yoga

like twice a week

its summer

i've got my head on
backwards

it's time to fucking party

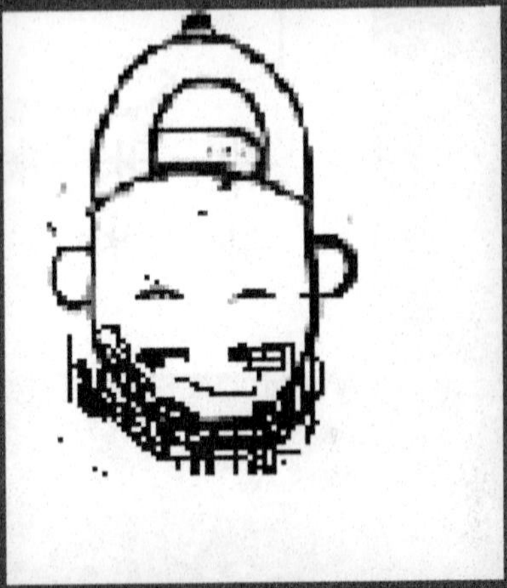

oh My God

ice is slippery

ISIS

no, Ice is

oh my God

there's a fire

i'm just cooking

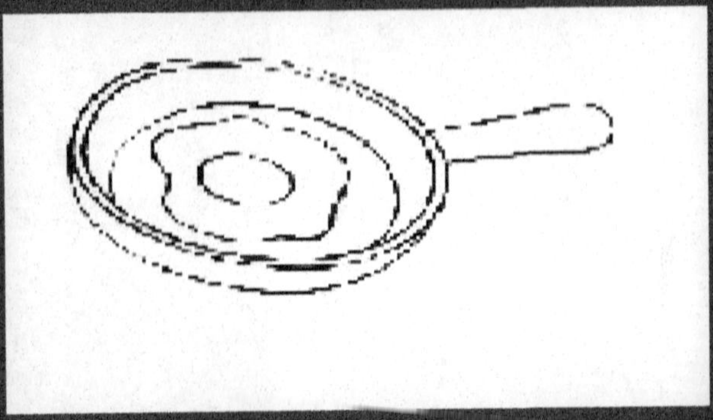

are you a smoke detector

that's what I thought

don't fuck with me

i've got power in me

benjamin tables are for glasses

not assess

i'm so glad to be home

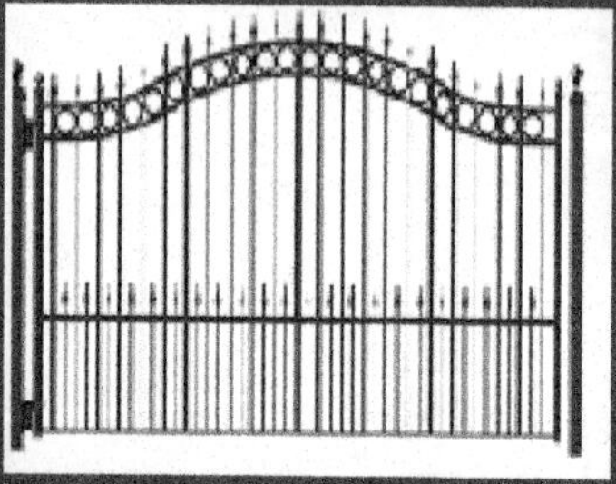

i'm kidding

i don't live there

you got to pay $500 and 1 penny

but I've only got $500

you've got what

i neeed

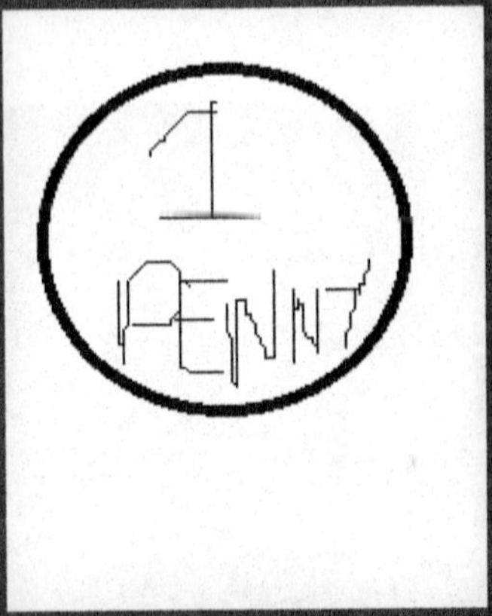

my horn doesn't work

so what

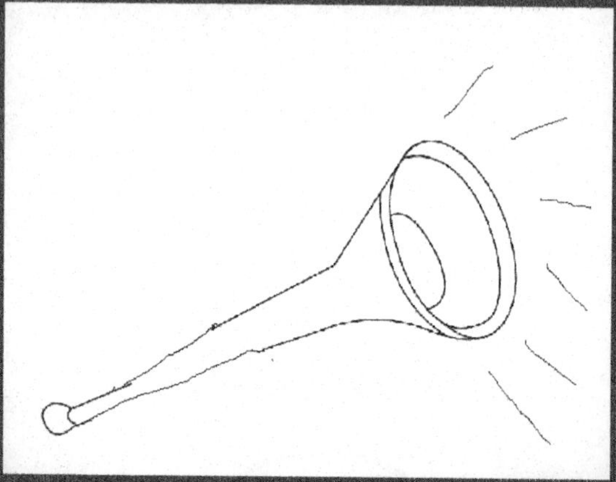

poooh

c'mon let's go

it's a green light

you ready

catch

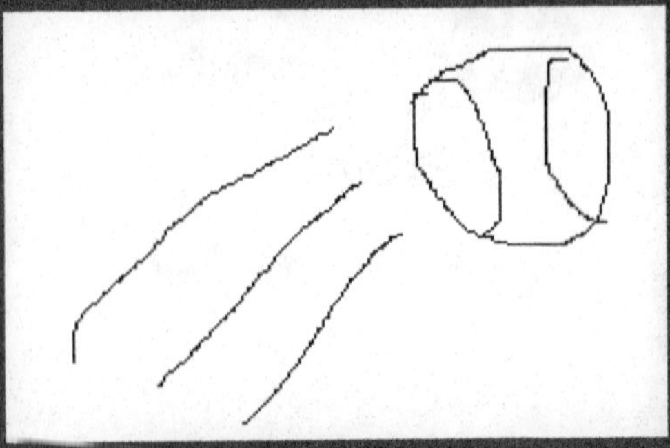

whoohoo

dude, what you doing

it's October 31st

homework today has two
questions
each one has 26 parts

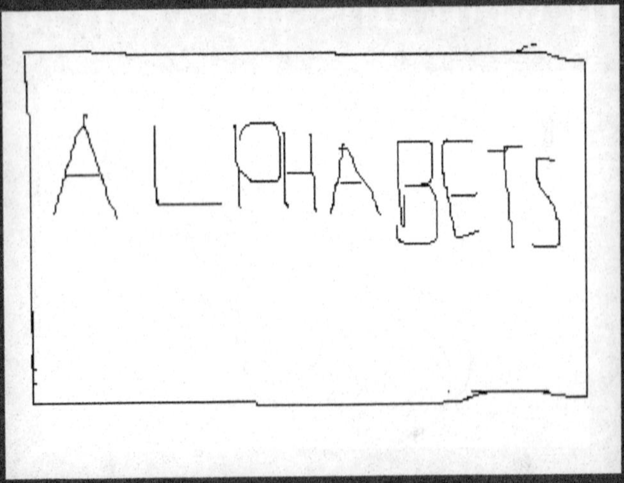

Oh Gosh

dad can you drive me to the movies

why can't you be like Kevin

your friend

kevin went missing yesterday

i'm a hard worker

uhuh

a lawyer

uhuh

are you listening

WHAT

okay i will put this here

daddy

stopppp

hey

why you lying down

like you pay them bills

hey girl

you should go out with me

i only date hot guys

what are thoossee

they are my crocs

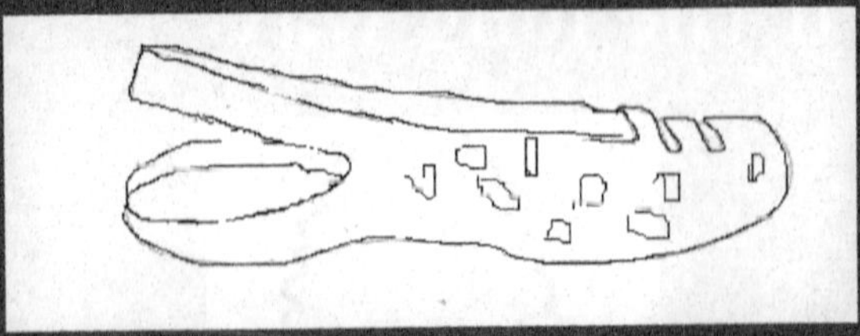

i like corn better

off the cob

i don't know

i like it the long way

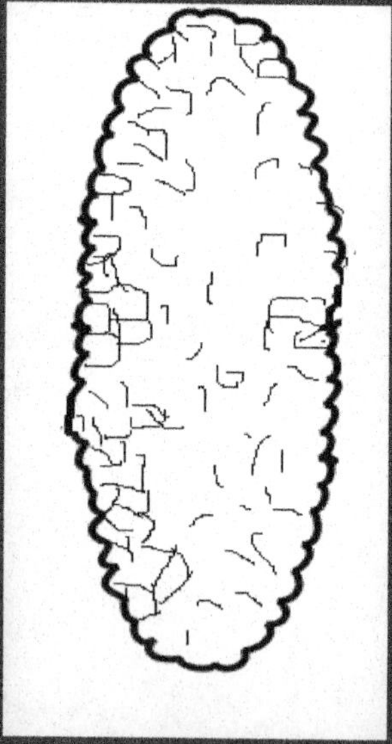

No

hurricane katrina

more like hurricane tortilla

i'm in my mum's car

vroom vroom

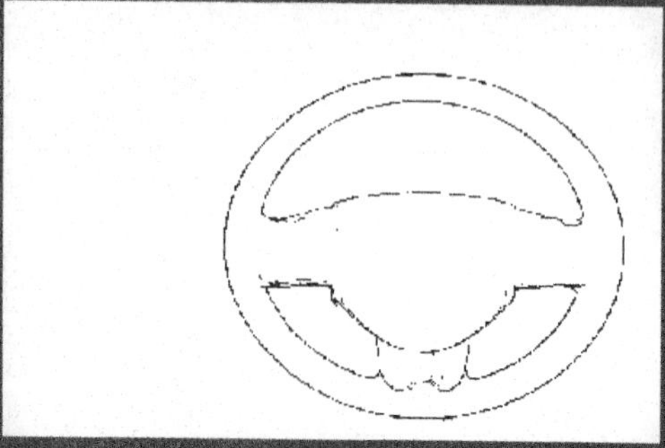

get out me car

noo

i brought you frankinscence

thank you

and I brought you myrrh

murder

i got you a valentine's day present

i told you I was on a diet

get out

why would you get me chocolate

my eye brows

bring all the guys

to my page

and they are like what's on
your face

that was legitness

Yeah that was

yeah mum

i'm in love

with this girl

imma introduce you to her

i'm washing me

and my cloth bitch(bath tub)

hey Jim

(wine)

have you seen your father

i've never met my father

mcdonalds turns me on

oh yes, yes, yes

Thank You

Thank you for taking your time to Read our Tribute to the late and Great Vine (R.I.P). We wish to use this medium to thank all the Viners who Created this wonderful Content for us to watch and laugh our f*cking ass out, (*try not to Laugh or grin*).

And the Creators of Vine for Providing us with this Platform of expression.

Acknowledgement

Our Appreciation goes to the creators of this vines, you guys Rock. Credits goes to the following:

Kayla Newman

king bach

nick colletti,

Michael LoPriore

Curtis Lepore

Jordan Burt

Nash Grier

Brittany Furlan

Rudy Mancuso

Jessi Smiles

Logan Paul

Simone Shepherd

Manon Mathews

Rachel Pike

Joshau Holz & Daniel Lara

Brandon Williams

Liz Schreiber

Jada Reilee

Bryan Silva

Christine Sydelko

Gasoleen

Jessi Lockett

Adam Perkins

Anthony Padilla

Josh Kennedy

Katie Ryan

Sexylexy

Peaches Monroe

Evan Breen

Gucci POPTART

Joshua Kravchenko

ben taylor… etc

N:B: if you feel, there is anyone who was left out in this acknowledgement. You can help us by sending to us the vine and the creator name, so we can give credits where due.

Thanks !!!

Thanks for Creating these Masterpiece that spread through this amazing platform. Although, we'll miss vine. This Book, the vine and her milk is truly a delight for the sensations, bringing back the riveting quotes we all laughed at together as a united internet community. Keep the fire of true comedy ablaze in your home By Getting a Copy of This Book.

Thanks So Much For The Support. If you Enjoyed the vine and her milk.

Take a Little Time to Leave Us A Review. It will be very much appreciated!

One or Two Statement Will Go a Long Way in Helping Other People Looking to Buy.

Follow Us on Facebook Here>>

https://www.facebook.com/vineandhoney

Instagram Here:

Instagram @vineandhoney

Send Us Feedback Via >>
info@vineandhoney.com

CPSIA information can be obtained
at www.ICGtesting.com
Printed in the USA
BVOW06s1930010118
504133BV00012B/321/P

9 781948 191135